PAUL SHIELDS

Mountain Biking in Idaho

Exploring the various mountain bike locations throughout the state of Idaho.

Copyright © 2023 by Paul Shields

All rights reserved. No part of this publication may be reproduced, stored or transmitted in any form or by any means, electronic, mechanical, photocopying, recording, scanning, or otherwise without written permission from the publisher. It is illegal to copy this book, post it to a website, or distribute it by any other means without permission.

Paul Shields asserts the moral right to be identified as the author of this work.

Paul Shields has no responsibility for the persistence or accuracy of URLs for external or third-party Internet Websites referred to in this publication and does not guarantee that any content on such Websites is, or will remain, accurate or appropriate.

Designations used by companies to distinguish their products are often claimed as trademarks. All brand names and product names used in this book and on its cover are trade names, service marks, trademarks and registered trademarks of their respective owners. The publishers and the book are not associated with any product or vendor mentioned in this book. None of the companies referenced within the book have endorsed the book.

First edition

This book was professionally typeset on Reedsy.
Find out more at reedsy.com

Contents

1	Introduction	1
2	The Allure of Mountain Biking in Idaho	4
3	Essential Gear and Preparations	7
4	Boise and the Treasure Valley	12
5	Sun Valley and the Wood River Valley	15
6	The Magic Valley	19
7	The Sawtooth National Recreation Area	22
8	North Idaho and the Panhandle	25
9	East Idaho and the Teton Valley	28
10	Responsible Riding and Trail Etiquette	31
11	Conclusion	34
12	Resources	36

1

Introduction

Idaho Mountain Biking: Unveiling the Gem State's Best Trails

Welcome to the Gem State, where adventure meets the great outdoors and mountain biking dreams come true. Idaho has vast and diverse landscapes that are a haven for mountain biking enthusiasts seeking adrenaline-pumping challenges, breathtaking vistas, and unforgettable riding experiences. From the northern panhandle to the southern border, from the Sawtooth Mountains to the Treasure Valley, Idaho offers an array of trails that inspire and test riders of all skill levels. "Idaho Mountain Biking" is your comprehensive guide to the state's finest mountain biking trails.

Whether you're an experienced rider with countless miles under your belt or a newcomer eager to embark on a two-wheeled adventure, this book is your key to unlocking the hidden gems of the Gem State. Within these pages, we'll traverse the landscape revealing the best trails that Idaho has to offer. We'll take you on a journey through lush forests, across rugged canyons, and up challenging climbs that culminate in awe-inspiring views of the northwest. Our goal is to immerse you in the beauty and thrill of Idaho's mountain biking paradise.

A Diverse Playground for Mountain Bikers

Idaho's allure is as diverse as its geography. From the dense forests of the Boise foothills to the high alpine trails of Sun Valley, the arid magic of the City of Rocks and the scenery of the Sawtooth Mountains. Idaho trails cater to every taste and skill level and is a place where you can embrace the thrill of a technical descent, the solitude of a pristine single track, or the camaraderie of a bike park.

As we embark on this journey, we'll explore the unique charm and challenges of each region. You'll discover Boise and the Treasure Valley which is renowned for the accessibility of trails and vibrant biking communities. Sun Valley and the Wood River Valley possess some of the most iconic rides and stunning landscapes. The Magic Valley has its surprises, while the Sawtooth National Recreation Area, is a mountain biker's dream backdrop. North Idaho and the Panhandle offer diversity and enchantment. East Idaho and the Teton Valley, a lesser-known treasure.

Your Guide to Idaho's Mountain Biking Paradise

This book is your trusty companion, designed to equip you with the knowledge and inspiration needed to embark on your own Idaho mountain biking adventure. We'll cover the essential gear, safety, and preparations to ensure you're well-prepared for the varied trails. We'll discuss the unique characteristics and challenges of each region and introduce the standout trails that define them. Whether you're seeking a thrilling downhill ride, a technical challenge, or a scenic escape, Idaho's trails have you covered.

INTRODUCTION

Unlocking the Gem State's Best Trails

Get ready to explore the trails that have captured the hearts of riders from all over. Throughout the entire state, there's an Idaho trail waiting for you to conquer it. Join us as we unveil the hidden treasures that will inspire your next mountain biking journey in the Gem State.

So, saddle up, prepare your bike, and get ready to experience Idaho's Mountain Biking Paradise. Your next great adventure begins here.

2

The Allure of Mountain Biking in Idaho

In the heart of the American West, Idaho stands as a testament to nature's grandeur. Known as the Gem State, Idaho's landscapes are nothing short of spectacular. With its towering mountains, pristine lakes, lush forests, and rugged canyons, this state serves as a canvas for outdoor enthusiasts seeking adventures in their purest form. Among these enthusiasts, mountain bikers have discovered an adventure with challenging trails, breathtaking vistas, and a unique sense of adventure. In this chapter, we expose the allure of mountain biking in Idaho and what sets it apart as a premier destination for riders of all levels.

Diverse Terrain Beckons

Idaho's landscape is as diverse as it is extensive. To the north, the state shares its borders with the rugged and forested panhandle where the Selkirk Mountains stretch into Canada. In the south, the Snake River Plain offers a contrasting landscape of wide, arid expanses, punctuated by the striking Sawtooth Mountains and a multitude of pristine lakes. To the east, the Teton Range's jagged peaks tower over the expansive

Teton Valley. The verdant Boise foothills lead to the deep canyons of the Snake River. This geographical diversity offers mountain bikers a stunning array of terrain to explore, from high alpine trails to rolling desert singletracks.

A Unique Sense of Adventure

Mountain biking is more than a sport; it's a lifestyle that brings riders closer to nature and challenges them to push their boundaries. Idaho encapsulates this sense of adventure, with its remote and unspoiled landscapes that inspire exploration and discovery. The thrill of conquering technical descents, navigating rocky canyons, and ascending mountain passes keeps riders coming back for more. The sheer variety of trails and riding experiences in Idaho caters to everyone, from beginners looking for mellow rides to adrenaline junkies craving high-speed downhill descents.

A Growing Biking Community

Idaho's mountain biking community continues to grow and thrive. The state's unique allure attracts riders from all walks of life fostering a camaraderie that transcends age, skill level, and background. Local riding clubs and organizations work tirelessly to maintain and improve the trails, ensuring that riders have access to well-maintained routes that are both safe and enjoyable.

What Awaits in the Chapters Ahead

In the coming chapters, we will embark on a journey through Idaho's diverse regions, each offering unique mountain biking experiences. The bustling trails of Boise and the Treasure Valley and beyond to the iconic routes of Sun Valley and the Wood River Valley offer a variety of trails for all levels. The Magic Valley's enchanting trails and the Sawtooth National Recreation Area's rugged beauty provide diverse riding opportunities for all skill levels. Let's not forget about Northern Idaho and the Panhandle in addition to some lesser-known treasures of Eastern Idaho and the Teton Valley, we'll explore the best trails that the Gem State has to offer.

Our goal is to immerse you in the beauty and thrill of Idaho's mountain biking paradise, whether you're an experienced rider or a newcomer eager to start your adventure. In the information to follow, you'll find insights into the essential gear and preparations needed for the trails, the importance of trail etiquette, and responsible riding. Some personal stories from local riders of Idaho's trails that have deeply influenced my trail decisions have led to some of the most exciting adventures that I've had on my bike.

Prepare to unlock the hidden gems of the Gem State, where mountain biking dreams come true. As you venture through the following chapters, may the allure of Idaho's mountain biking paradise become your own, inspiring your next two-wheeled journey through this magnificent state.

3

Essential Gear and Preparations

Before you embark on your mountain biking adventure in Idaho, it's crucial to be well-prepared. The right gear and proper preparations can make the difference between a thrilling and safe ride and a potentially challenging or even dangerous experience. In this chapter, I'll provide some key aspects of gearing up for a successful mountain biking expedition in the Gem State.

Over many years of riding, the pack that I carry with me has become heavier to account for many possible scenarios. Although all items are suggestions, this is based on your skill level and the trails you decide to ride. Many trails are deeper into the mountains than others and some of the items are always necessary to carry each ride. But if do decide to carry many items, you can look at it as additional strength training carrying more weight!

Choosing the Right Bike for Idaho's Varied Terrain

Idaho's diverse terrain requires a bike that can handle a wide range of conditions. When selecting your mountain bike, consider the following factors.

- **Bike Type.** Mountain bikes come in various types, including hardtail, full-suspension, and fat bikes. Each has its advantages. Hardtail bikes are versatile and suitable for most trails, while full-suspension bikes are ideal for rough terrain. Fat bikes with their oversized tires are perfect for riding on snow and sand.
- **Frame Material.** The material of your bike's frame affects its weight and durability. Aluminum frames are lightweight and affordable, while carbon fiber frames are even lighter but more expensive. Steel frames are known for their durability and a smooth ride, though they can be heavier.
- **Wheel Size.** The choice between 27.5-inch (650b) and 29-inch wheels largely depends on your riding style. Smaller wheels provide better agility, while larger wheels roll over obstacles more easily and maintain momentum. The personal recommendation if you don't know is to opt for the larger 29-inch tires as these are more adaptable and comfortable for all rides.
- **Components.** The quality of your bike's components, including the drivetrain, brakes, and suspension, significantly impacts your riding experience. High-quality components offer better performance and durability.
- **Fit.** Ensure that your bike is the right size for your body and that it's properly adjusted. An ill-fitting bike can lead to discomfort, reduced control, and even injury.
- **Test Rides.** If possible, test ride several bikes to determine which one feels most comfortable and suits your riding style.

Safety Gear and Accessories

ESSENTIAL GEAR AND PREPARATIONS

Mountain biking can be exhilarating, but it's not without its risks. Safety should always be a top priority, and the right gear can make a significant difference in protecting you on the trail. Here's what you need:

- **Helmet.** A properly fitted and certified mountain biking helmet is non-negotiable. It's your first line of defense in case of a fall. Look for helmets with adequate ventilation and comfortable padding. The newest technology with MIPS (Multi-directional Impact Protection) has been very comfortable for me.
- **Gloves.** Quality mountain biking gloves provide a better grip on the handlebars, protect your hands from trail debris, and can reduce the severity of scrapes and abrasions in the event of a fall.
- **Protective Gear.** Depending on your style of riding, you may want to consider additional protective gear such as knee and elbow pads, as well as body armor. These provide added protection against impacts. These are items that I carry in my pack and are used for downhill riding as this is where I've had most of my falls.
- **Eyewear.** Sunglasses or clear lenses are essential to shield your eyes from branches, dust, and flying debris. They also help improve visibility in various lighting conditions.
- **Hydration System.** Staying hydrated is crucial during a ride. Consider a hydration pack with a built-in water reservoir or a water bottle cage on your bike to ensure you have access to fluids. This is a huge consideration, and you should take the necessary time to research and purchase. Be sure to get all the features possible. If you enjoy longer rides, get the biggest hydration pack you can comfortably carry.
- **Clothing.** Dress appropriately for the weather and your riding conditions. Moisture-wicking, breathable clothing is essential. Padded shorts can enhance comfort, especially on longer rides. Although it may not be cool enough for a jacket when you start your

ride, it's a good idea to put a light jacket in your pack. The weather in Idaho can occasionally change quickly.

Pre-ride Maintenance

Before you hit the trails, it's essential to ensure your bike is in good working order. Regular maintenance will keep your bike safe and reliable. Here are some key areas to check.

- **Tires.** Verify tire pressure and examine the condition of your tires. Properly inflated tires are crucial for grip and control. Inspect them for signs of wear or damage.
- **Brakes.** Ensure that your brakes are functioning correctly. Check the brake pads for wear and replace them if necessary. For bikes with hydraulic brakes, consider bleeding the system if you notice a decrease in performance. Unless you know the proper technique for this, I'd suggest taking your bike to a local bike shop to do it.
- **Lubrication.** Keep your chain and drivetrain well-lubricated to reduce friction and extend the life of your components. A clean and properly lubricated chain improves shifting and reduces wear.
- **Suspension Setup.** Adjust your suspension to match the terrain and your riding style. Refer to your bike's manual or seek professional help if needed. Proper suspension setup can significantly impact your comfort and control on the trail.
- **Tighten Bolts.** Regularly check and tighten bolts, especially on critical components like the stem, handlebars, saddle, and pedals. Loose bolts can lead to accidents and damage to your bike.
- **Safety Check.** Verify that your bike's quick releases, levers, and safety features are functioning as intended. Ensure that your brakes are responsive, and your gears shift smoothly.

By investing in the right gear and maintaining your bike, you enhance your safety and overall enjoyment on the trails. Proper gear and a well-maintained bike will give you the confidence to tackle the challenging trails that the Idaho mountains offer. In the chapters ahead, we'll review in more detail the specifics of mountain biking, explore the best trails across Idaho, and provide tips for responsible and enjoyable riding.

4

Boise and the Treasure Valley

The Treasure Valley, anchored by the vibrant city of Boise, offers mountain biking enthusiasts a rich tapestry of trails and riding experiences. Known for its accessibility and diverse terrain, this region is a fantastic starting point for those eager to explore the Gem State's mountains. In this chapter, we'll look at the versatility of trails in Boise and the surrounding Treasure Valley, showcasing trails that cater to riders of all levels and riding preferences.

Military Reserve Park

Nestled on the northern edge of Boise, Military Reserve Park is a mountain biking haven. This multi-use park features a network of trails that meander through picturesque foothills, offering breathtaking views of the city below. It's an excellent destination for riders of all skill levels, from beginners seeking a gentle introduction to the sport to seasoned riders looking for a quick ride close to the city.

Highlights:

- Crestline Trail: A favorite among local riders, this trail offers a mix of smooth singletrack and rocky sections with beautiful views of the city and the surrounding hills.
- Three Bears Loop: A moderately challenging loop with rewarding climbs and descents, featuring three distinct climbs known as the "Three Bears".

Bogus Basin

Just a short drive from Boise, Bogus Basin is about 16 miles from the valley. It is a year-round mountain recreation area that transforms into a mountain biking area during the warmer months. With a range of trails that all riders can find a trail to their liking, it's a fantastic place to explore the beauty of the Boise National Forest. There is a chair lift that is operational on the weekends to take you to the top of the mountain.

Highlights:

- Around the Mountain: This trail is great if you are an intermediate/advanced rider. It is about 9 miles long and offers great views into the Treasure Valley and Boise National Forest.
- Shafer Butte Trail: This trail offers riders stunning alpine scenery, with wildflowers in the summer and excellent views of the surrounding mountains.
- Mahalo Trail: A downhill flow trail that provides a thrilling experience with jumps, berms, and technical sections.

Ada/Eagle Bike Park

Located in nearby Eagle, Idaho, the Ada/Eagle Bike Park is a playground for mountain bikers. This purpose-built park offers a variety of trails, making it an ideal destination for riders who want to test their skills on jumps, berms, and technical features.

This is not limited to jumps and berms. This area offers some inclines and declines that will prepare you for longer climbs. The ascents on the trails go up to the top of the same mountain and make for a tough climb but isn't a long climb.

Highlights:

- Ada BMX: A pump track and jump park for riders of all skill levels, with progressive features for beginners to experts.
- Eagle Bike Park Trails: A range of trails suitable for various skill levels, including technical descents and challenging climbs.

The Boise Experience

Boise and the Treasure Valley provide an accessible and exciting mountain biking experience that riders of all levels and preferences will enjoy. Whether you're seeking scenic rides in the foothills, downhill thrills at Bogus Basin, or technical challenges at the Ada/Eagle Bike Park, this region has it all. The community of local riders is welcoming and enthusiastic making it easy to find like-minded individuals to share your biking adventures.

As you explore Boise and the Treasure Valley, take time to soak in the incredible vistas and immerse yourself in the unique landscape that Idaho offers. In the chapters that follow, we'll continue our journey through the Gem State, unveiling more of its best mountain biking trails, so you can fully experience mountain biking in Idaho.

5

Sun Valley and the Wood River Valley

Sun Valley and the Wood River Valley are renowned for their stunning landscapes, world-class skiing, and of course, exceptional mountain biking opportunities. Nestled in central Idaho, this region offers riders a unique blend of alpine beauty and challenging trails. In this chapter, we'll explore the iconic mountain biking destinations that make Sun Valley and the Wood River Valley a must-visit for any rider.

Bald Mountain Trails

Bald Mountain, known locally as "Baldy," is the crown jewel of the Sun Valley region. During the summer months, the ski slopes transform into an epicenter for mountain biking. Riders of all levels can experience the breathtaking vistas, wildflower-covered hillsides, and exhilarating descents that this mountain has to offer.

Highlights:

- Warm Springs Trail: An iconic downhill route known for its technical challenges and thrilling descents. This trail takes you from the top of Bald Mountain down to Warm Springs Creek.
- White Cloud Trails: A network of scenic trails that wind through the beautiful White Clouds, offering a variety of options for different skill levels.

Adams Gulch Trails

The Adams Gulch area, located just north of Ketchum, is a paradise for riders looking to explore the serene beauty of the Wood River Valley. The trails here cater to a wide range of abilities, with options for mellow rides and technical challenges.

Highlights:

- Bald Mountain to Adams Gulch Loop: A classic loop that combines the stunning vistas of Bald Mountain with the peaceful beauty of

Adams Gulch.

- Cow Creek Trail: A moderate trail with a gradual ascent through a picturesque aspen grove, leading to rewarding panoramic views.

Fisher Creek Loop

Located in the heart of the Sawtooth National Recreation Area, the Fisher Creek Loop is an unforgettable adventure for mountain biking enthusiasts. The loop takes riders through pristine wilderness, offering a mix of challenging climbs, technical descents, and scenic beauty that's hard to beat.

Highlights:

- Fisher Creek Trail: A rugged singletrack that provides technical challenges and incredible scenery as it winds through the forest.
- Boundary Creek to Atlanta: A point-to-point ride with stunning mountain views, deep forest, and a memorable descent into the historic town of Atlanta.

Sun Valley and the Wood River Valley are renowned not only for their exceptional mountain biking trails but also for their natural beauty and vibrant communities. With such diverse riding opportunities and stunning alpine scenery, Sun Valley is an amazing region for mountain biking enthusiasts.

In the chapters to come, we'll continue our journey through Idaho's mountain biking locations, exploring the diverse regions that make the Gem State a premier destination for riders of all levels. Saddle up, prepare your bike, and get ready to experience the next thrilling trail that awaits in the Gem State.

MOUNTAIN BIKING IN IDAHO

6

The Magic Valley

The Magic Valley, with its captivating landscapes and diverse terrain, offers a hidden treasure trove of mountain biking opportunities. This region includes cities like Twin Falls and Jerome, which are not as well-known as Sun Valley or Boise. The unique charm and distinct riding experiences here get overlooked. In this chapter, we'll explore the trails and adventures that await in the Magic Valley.

Auger Falls

Auger Falls, located near Twin Falls, is a gem for mountain bikers seeking scenic and moderately challenging trails. The area features the Snake River Canyon and offers riders the chance to explore a variety of terrains, from winding desert singletracks to exposed ridge rides.

Highlights:

- Auger Falls Loop: A moderately challenging loop that winds along the canyon rim, offering incredible views of the Snake River.

- Shoshone Falls: For those looking for a unique experience, the trail around Shoshone Falls provide technical challenges and a backdrop of the "Niagara of the West."

Castle Rocks State Park

Castle Rocks State Park, situated near Almo offers mountain biking opportunities against a backdrop of unique rock formations. Riders can explore a network of trails that lead to interesting geological features and stunning vistas. This is also a unique place to camp and rock climb.

Highlights:

- Wings of Fire: A popular trail that winds through the Castle Rocks and City of Rocks formations, offering a mix of technical challenges and beautiful scenery.
- Table Rock Loop: A longer loop that takes riders on a journey through the unique landscapes of Castle Rocks State Park.

City of Rocks National Reserve

The neighboring City of Rocks National Reserve is another fantastic destination for mountain bikers. Known for its intriguing rock formations and rich history, this area provides a wide range of riding experiences, from mellow scenic routes to technical challenges.

Highlights:

- Almo Loop Trail: This loop offers a mix of desert riding and fascinating rock formations, with opportunities to explore the unique landscapes of the reserve.
- Flaming Rock Loop: A moderate trail that takes riders through the reserve's striking geological features.

The Magic Valley may not be as widely recognized as some of Idaho's more famous mountain biking destinations, but it holds a unique allure. With its stunning geological formations, desert landscapes, and challenging trails, it's a region that every mountain biker should explore.

In the chapters to come, we'll continue our journey through Idaho's mountain biking paradise, uncovering more of the state's best trails and the diverse riding experiences they offer. Prepare for your next adventure in the Gem State as we explore additional regions and their captivating landscapes.

7

The Sawtooth National Recreation Area

The Sawtooth National Recreation Area, nestled in the heart of Idaho, is a mountain biker's dream come true. With its towering peaks, crystal-clear lakes, and pristine wilderness, this region offers some of the most stunning and challenging mountain biking experiences in the Gem State. In this chapter, we'll outline some captivating trails that await adventurous riders in the Sawtooth National Recreation Area.

Fisher Creek Loop

The Fisher Creek Loop is a premier trail within the Sawtooth National Recreation Area offering riders an unforgettable adventure. The loop takes you through some of the most pristine wilderness Idaho has to offer, complete with technical challenges and breathtaking scenery.

Highlights:

- Fisher Creek Trail: A rugged singletrack that provides a thrilling mix of technical challenges and stunning alpine beauty.

- Boundary Creek to Atlanta: A point-to-point ride where riders will reap the rewards of the climb with incredible mountain vistas, lush forests, and a memorable descent into the historic town of Atlanta.

Redfish Lake to Stanley

Redfish Lake is a jewel in the Sawtooth Mountains, and the trail connecting it to the nearby town of Stanley offers riders an unparalleled alpine experience. The ride provides stunning views, technical descents, and a sense of being fully immersed in the wilderness.

Highlights:

- Redfish Lake to Stanley Trail: A point-to-point ride that takes you through the heart of the Sawtooth Mountains offering challenging climbs and thrilling descents that end up in the charming town of Stanley.

Grandjean to Stanley

This trail follows the Payette River and offers riders a chance to experience the Sawtooth National Recreation Area from a different perspective. It's a more mellow route compared to some of the more technical trails in the area, making it accessible to a wider range of riders.

Highlights:

- Grandjean to Stanley Trail: A scenic route that winds along the Payette River, allowing riders to appreciate the unique beauty of the Sawtooth Mountains.

The Sawtooth National Recreation Area is a great experience for mountain bikers, providing a mix of challenging trails and stunning alpine vistas. As you explore this region, be prepared to be captivated by the rugged beauty of the Sawtooth Mountains and the thrill of the trails they hold.

In the chapters to come, we'll continue our journey through Idaho's trails, uncovering more of the state's best trails and the diverse riding experiences they offer. The Sawtooth National Recreation Area is just one of the remarkable regions that make Idaho a premier destination for riders of all levels.

8

North Idaho and the Panhandle

North Idaho and the Panhandle region offer mountain biking enthusiasts a diverse and enchanting range of riding opportunities. From the lively trails of Canfield Mountain to the gravity-fueled fun at Silver Mountain Bike Park and the historic Route of the Hiawatha, this region is a true treasure for riders of all levels. In this chapter, we'll talk about the unique mountain biking experiences that await in North Idaho and the Panhandle.

Canfield Mountain

Nestled in the heart of Coeur d'Alene, Canfield Mountain offers an extensive network of trails for riders to explore. This area is well-loved for its accessibility, technical challenges, and breathtaking scenery.

Highlights:

- Canfield Mountain Trail System: A network of trails that cater to a wide range of skill levels, offering scenic vistas, rocky descents, and plenty of challenges.

- XC Loop: A popular cross-country loop featuring a mix of climbs, descents, and technical sections.

Silver Mountain Bike Park

Silver Mountain Bike Park, located in Kellogg, is a gravity rider's paradise. It features a gondola-serviced bike park with a variety of downhill and freeride trails, making it a thrilling destination for riders looking for gravity-fueled adventures.

Highlights:

- Galena Ridge Trail: A downhill trail with technical features, jumps, and berms that provide a thrilling experience for experienced riders.
- Lower Basin Trail: A flowing, beginner-friendly trail that's perfect for those new to downhill riding.

Route of the Hiawatha

The Route of the Hiawatha is a historic rail-to-trail adventure that takes riders through some of the most beautiful and remote parts of the Idaho Panhandle. The trail offers a unique combination of history and mountain biking, with several tunnels and trestles along the way.

Highlights:

- Taft Tunnel: At 1.7 miles long, the Taft Tunnel is a highlight of the trail and a memorable experience for riders.
- St. Paul Pass: Known as the "longest railroad bridge in the world," this trestle provides stunning views and a sense of riding through history.

North Idaho and the Panhandle region provide a mix of technical challenges and gravity-fueled excitement, making it a captivating destination for mountain biking enthusiasts. As you explore this area, you'll encounter diverse landscapes, history, and a welcoming community of riders eager to share their passion for the sport.

We'll continue our journey through Idaho's mountain biking opportunities, uncovering more of the state's best trails and the diverse riding experiences they offer. North Idaho and the Panhandle are just one facet of the remarkable regions that make Idaho a premier destination for riders of all levels.

9

East Idaho and the Teton Valley

East Idaho and the Teton Valley, an often lesser-known treasure for mountain bikers, provide a wealth of riding opportunities against a backdrop of stunning landscapes. This region offers riders a unique blend of rugged mountain terrain, alpine vistas, and serene trails. In this chapter, we'll point out the captivating mountain biking experiences that await in East Idaho and the Teton Valley.

Grand Targhee Resort

Grand Targhee Resort, located near Driggs, Idaho, is a mountain biking haven with a focus on lift-serviced riding. The resort provides access to a network of trails catering to riders of all levels, from beginners to experts.

Highlights:

- Rick's Basin Trail: A scenic and beginner-friendly trail offering stunning views and a taste of Targhee's alpine beauty.
- Steady Eddy Trail: A flowy, intermediate trail known for its smooth

descents, jumps, and berms.

South Fork of the Teton River

The South Fork of the Teton River area near Victor, Idaho, provides a serene escape for mountain bikers looking to immerse themselves in the beauty of the Teton Valley. The trails here offer a mix of natural beauty and moderate riding challenges.

Highlights:

- South Fork of the Teton River Trail: A picturesque trail that follows the river, offering a sense of tranquility and a delightful ride through pristine landscapes.

Caribou-Targhee National Forest

The Caribou-Targhee National Forest, a vast expanse of wilderness in East Idaho, is a playground for mountain bikers eager to explore the rugged terrain and alpine beauty of the Teton Range.

Highlights:

- Mesa Falls Scenic Byway: A scenic route with access to multiple trails, including the Mesa Falls Mountain Bike Trail, offering riders a blend of alpine scenery and technical challenges.
- Big Elk Creek Trail: A moderately challenging trail that meanders through the forest and offers riders a serene experience in the wilderness.

East Idaho and the Teton Valley are hidden gems for mountain biking enthusiasts, offering a unique blend of serene trails, alpine vistas, and rugged terrain. As you explore this region, you'll have the opportunity to immerse yourself in the pristine wilderness and enjoy a sense of adventure that's truly unique to the Gem State.

We'll continue our journey through Idaho's mountain biking trail system, uncovering more of the state's best trails and the diverse riding experiences they offer. East Idaho and the Teton Valley are just one facet of the remarkable regions that make Idaho a premier destination for riders of all levels.

10

Responsible Riding and Trail Etiquette

Mountain biking in Idaho's diverse and stunning landscapes is a privilege that comes with responsibilities. As stewards of the trails, every rider needs to practice responsible riding and adhere to trail etiquette to ensure the trails are enjoyable for everyone. In this chapter, we'll outline some of the principles of responsible riding and the etiquette that helps preserve the beauty of Idaho's vast trail system for generations to come.

Leave No Trace

"Leave No Trace" is a guiding principle for all outdoor activities, including mountain biking. It emphasizes minimizing the impact on the environment and respecting the natural beauty of the trails. The following are several key principles that all trail users should adhere to.

- Plan and Prepare: Before hitting the trail, plan your route, check weather conditions, and ensure you have the necessary gear and supplies.
- Travel and Camp on Durable Surfaces: Stay on designated trails to

avoid damaging the fragile ecosystems. Don't create new trails or cut switchbacks.
- Dispose of Waste Properly: Pack out all trash, including gel wrappers and energy bar remnants. If nature calls, use a restroom facility or a portable waste disposal system.
- Leave What You Find: Preserve the natural environment by not picking plants, disturbing wildlife, or altering the landscape. Leave rocks, flowers, and historical artifacts where you found them.
- Minimize Campfire Impact: Mountain biking doesn't often involve campfires, but if you do camp, use a camp stove for cooking and adhere to fire regulations.
- Respect Wildlife: Observe animals from a distance and avoid disturbing them. Give them space to ensure their safety and comfort.

Trail Etiquette

Mountain bikers share the trails with hikers, equestrians, and other outdoor enthusiasts. Adhering to trail etiquette helps maintain a positive and safe environment for everyone.

- Yield the Trail: When encountering hikers and equestrians, yield the trail to them. Slow down, announce your presence, and be courteous. Uphill riders have the right of way.
- Stay in Control: Maintain control of your bike, especially on descents. Excessive speed can pose a danger to yourself and others. This is especially important on a trail that may have blind corners.
- Announce Yourself: Use a friendly greeting or bell to announce your approach when overtaking slower trail users. This prevents surprises and ensures safe passing.
- Respect Trail Closures: Be aware of trail closures or restrictions, which may be in place to protect wildlife, sensitive habitats, or for

other reasons. Always adhere to posted regulations.
- Stay on the Trail: Avoid cutting switchbacks or creating new trails. Stay on designated routes to minimize environmental impact.
- Group Riding: Ride single file on narrow trails, and don't block the trail when stopping to rest or wait for others.
- Be Mindful of Wildlife: Keep a respectful distance from wildlife, and do not disturb or feed them. It's essential for their well-being and safety.
- Share the Trail: Remember that you're sharing the trail with a diverse community of outdoor enthusiasts. Respect their right to enjoy the natural beauty of the area.

By practicing these principles and trail etiquette, mountain bikers can help preserve the pristine beauty of Idaho's mountain bike trails. Responsible riding ensures that the trails remain enjoyable for all, maintains the ecological integrity of the wilderness, and fosters a positive and inclusive outdoor community.

In the final chapter to come, we'll wrap up our journey through the Gem State's Mountain biking, summarizing the highlights of each region and offering some parting thoughts and advice for riders of all levels.

11

Conclusion

As we conclude our journey through Idaho's Mountain Biking Adventures and some of the best trails, we've embarked on an adventure through the diverse and breathtaking landscapes of the Gem State. From the foothills of Boise to the alpine splendor of the Sawtooth Mountains, the rugged terrain of North Idaho, and the tranquil beauty of East Idaho, we've explored the remarkable trails and experiences that await mountain biking enthusiasts.

Idaho's mountain biking paradise isn't just a collection of trails; it's an invitation to connect with the natural world, challenge your limits, and experience the thrill of adventure. It's a place where riders of all levels can find their little piece of Idaho that they love all while on two wheels.

Throughout our journey, we've learned about the diverse terrain, essential gear, and responsible riding practices that make Idaho a premier destination for mountain biking. We've encountered iconic trails and hidden gems, gravity-fueled fun and serene rides, and the unique beauty of each region.

CONCLUSION

But the true essence of this paradise lies not just in the trails themselves, but in the community of riders who call Idaho home. It's in the camaraderie that forms at trailheads, the shared stories of epic rides, and the common love for the outdoors. It's in the dedication of volunteers who maintain and protect the trails, and in the respect for the land and its inhabitants.

As you prepare for your adventures in Idaho's mountain biking trail system, remember the principles of responsible riding and trail etiquette. By respecting the environment and fellow trail users, you contribute to the preservation of this unique paradise for future generations of riders to enjoy.

Whether you're a seasoned rider seeking technical challenges or a casual cyclist yearning for scenic vistas, Idaho offers something for everyone. Get out there and explore the diverse regions, and make the most of the Gem State's extraordinary trails.

May your pedals spin smoothly, your tires grip steadfastly, and your heart be filled with the joy of the ride. With each journey, you become part of the legacy of Idaho's mountain biking paradise—a legacy of adventure, respect, and boundless beauty.

Thank you for joining us on this exploration of Idaho's mountain biking adventure. May your future rides in this remarkable state be filled with unforgettable experiences and the thrill of the trail.

Happy riding!

If you found this book helpful, I'd be very appreciative if you left a positive review for the book on Amazon!

12

Resources

Portus, S. (2021, November 2). *What is MIPS, how does it work and is it really worth it?* BikeRadar. https://www.bikeradar.com/advice/buyers-guides/what-is-mips/

Bogus Basin. (2023, October 25). *Maps & Statistics | Bogus Basin.* https://bogusbasin.org/your-mountain/maps-statistics/

Idaho, A. (2023, October 30). *Department of Parks and Recreation.* Department of Parks and Recreation. https://parksandrecreation.idaho.gov/

General Trail Etiquette | Ridge to Rivers. (n.d.). https://www.ridgetorivers.org/etiquette/general-trail-etiquette/

Mountain biking. (2018, January 16). The Unofficial Website of Boise's Historic North End Neighborhood. https://northend.org/mountain-biking/

Visitsouthidaho. (2023, July 17). *Gooding's Little City of Rocks contains*

RESOURCES

many mysterious rock formations, ancient rock art; great place to go hiking. Visit Southern Idaho. https://visitsouthidaho.com/goodings-little-city-rocks-contains-many-mysterious-rock-formations-ancient-rock-art-great-place-go-hiking/

Made in the USA
Monee, IL
31 March 2025